# FINDING YOUR WAY

# FINDING YOUR WAY

*Single Parenthood
and the Path to
Personal Fulfillment*

AVERY NIGHTINGALE

Creative Quill Press

# CONTENTS

# CHAPTER 1

# Introduction

The number of single parent households has greatly increased over the years. There are 14 million single parents in America, only 1 in 6 take child support from their child's other parent, 1 in 3 receive public assistance (welfare), and 1 in 2 go without receiving money owed for the care of their child. The latter figures include my own life as well. While being a single parent automatically means being the sole provider of the household, there are still numerous misconceptions and generalizations about one's journey, both personally and parenting-wise. I myself have grown up in a single parent household and have also become a single parent. My life, as well as those of my parents, seemed to be on a continuous and repetitive tape. Since I had my very first daughter at the tender age of 16, my journey through life has been the difficult path of single parenthood; a road less traveled. Throughout my transition from child to single parent, I have come to learn a great number of life lessons; lessons that have proved to be my guiding beacons and personal markers.

With the recent advent of popular terms such as "single mom," "single dad," "single parent," and "deadbeat dad," society has made numerous generalizations and misconceptions in order to increase their claims of understanding and awareness about single parenting. Most of the time, there seems to be a display of support with statements such as single moms are "superwoman" and single dads are "superman." These single parents of today have been classified as heroes of today's society. There is also this notion that being a single parent alone means poverty, back child support and a life lived on and around welfare while being in and out of relationships. Celebrities who are single parents are paraded on magazines and talk shows as a form of inspiration. In certain situations, it can be quite charming. Sadly, reality isn't all that black and white.

# CHAPTER 2

# Understanding Single Parenthood

In this country, 35% of all children and 72% of African-American children are born to parents who are not married, although many parents are cohabitating with the biological parent. The U.S. Census Bureau counts these homes as ones led by a single parent, as do many social researchers. Pew research also adds one more element to the pool: people headed by two unmarried but cohabitating parents. Seventy-five percent of all children who live with two cohabitating parents are living with biological parents, compared to the 26% of cohabitating couples who have stepchildren. Women who find themselves suddenly single are more economically disadvantaged than men and are often given a disproportionate share of their overall income to their children, leaving them with less money to spend on themselves.

An overview of single parenthood comes from Dr. Elizabeth Marquardt, director of the Center for Marriage and Families of the Institute for American Values in New York City, NY. She explains that there are many ways for a single parent home to come about and many shades of parenting that we might think of as single, from never-married 20-somethings to mature widows or widowers and everyone in between. For any group, however, there are some common problems and attitudes that need to be examined.

### 2.1. Challenges Faced by Single Parents

PCC is based on the belief that building relationships through shared activities and celebrating belief in children supports parental reconstituted frozen belief in the child who is continually difficult to love. It also supports working with children to co-construct activities where the parent in turn is supported and celebrated, and so begins to address the absence of supportive adult relationships of the single parent. In their next section, we used the extensive empowerment evaluation framework promoted within the theory of this approach to illustrate the impact these conversations have on the lives of single parents and their children.

Single parents feel most challenged in managing everyday-ness. The internal strains include sleep deprivation, managing work and children through continual sickness, isolation, and financial pressure, the pressure that leads many mothers to conclude that "resilience simply can't be maintained with no emotional support of any kind". This chapter presents a particular approach to intervention that has been designed to address this stress. It is a form of individual, choice theory-based coaching called ParentChildConnect (PCC). PCC involves teaching parents to recognize and structure joyful interactions that are based on children's own strengths and interests.

The proportion of US single parent families is rising, and the majority report balancing work and family as their single greatest challenge. They feel stretched too thin and spreading themselves too wide, and yearning for a break. The reason single parents report that balance is their single greatest challenge is clear from taking their perspective. They feel all the responsibilities for daily child care (waking, dressing, feeding, comforting, bathing, managing illness, playing, insuring safety and attending Johnny's ball games) as well as the responsibility for home maintenance (providing clothing, feeding, and shelter) and paying the expense of raising children.

## 2.2. Embracing Single Parenthood

The literature provides a plethora of examples of the nurturing and caring characteristic of the Black family. Darder and Torres (2004) in discussing Vygotsky's construct of sociogenesis argue that the "process through which individuals evolve is central to the survival of the larger collective" (p. 33). They further argue that the process through which knowledge is shared and transmitted through memetic activity is a communal experience where "communities of memory and future possibility" interact to lend support to the individual. Storrs (1989) posits that "values and power relations flow from the larger society through the family and community and are internalized by individuals". Deyhle and LeCompte (1999) assert that the definition of community as being the "reinforcer of human purposes and meanings" (p. 194) is hardly a sentiment not endorsed in the Black community as Frohlick and Hazen (2002) suggest in their discussion of Yoruba childrearing practices.

What a difference a generation makes! I cherish and long for the days when, as a girl growing up in the Black community, I had a vast and wondrous array of "aunties" and "cousins" who were my great-grandmother, grandmother, mother's friends, and sisters of friends, among others, watching over me as I played in the yard or walking down the street or playing with other children in the area. At the sight of one of them, one was warned to exhibit good behavior. If one did not, their departure would indeed actually produce some visible consequences that would connect anger, annoyance, and/or embarrassment at the offending child, with some item being wielded as an emblem of the aunts' or cousins' disapproval. There are days when I wish for those times and worry not so much for myself but for the generations of adults and children to come who might never know the comfort that comes from being in the care of a parcel of women who, in spite of the challenges that each faced, tried to inculcate in their children values of self-worth, religious fundamentalism, and the desire to seek personal, professional, and economic fortuity.

# CHAPTER 3

# Nurturing Your Emotional Well-being

Feelings are reasons. They are feedback. They exist to convey information to you. It's important to notice when you are uncomfortable. Your feelings convey where there's room for improvement in your life or viewpoints. By breathing through discomfort, you are able to thoughtfully grow through it. When you do, you open yourself wide to your creative voice. Noticing unsettled feels tells you what you don't like, so you can set out to improve it. Noticing joyful feelings highlights what else excites you, calls you forward, and deserves more time. Feelings tell you what you love and what bums you out. They are crucial guides on your personal fulfillment track.

As your relationship changes, your center of gravity shifts. Compassion, understanding, intention, and grace are all part of striking off-road on an adventure of a lifetime with your favorite little people. Embrace the plasticity of your life and make purposeful, conscious decisions about with whom and what you fill your time. Navigate on common values. Be authentic. Be brave. Celebrate your successes. Be patient in growth and learning. Acknowledge your challenges.

Create impermeable bonds of loving friendship with yourself and the amazing person you're hanging out with all day every day. It'll be your greatest adventure yet! Making the most of your journey requires you to be a strong, calm, collected, nimble leader. To achieve this, nurturing your emotional well-being is priority number one. Validate your feelings, creative voice, and POV with discomfort. Know the different "views of you" as you relax in, narrate politely over, and, depending on the day, have pride in the development of your fill-in-the-blank skills, quality of character, practice areas, and the one to rule them all, self.

Appreciating things is a good way to cultivate an attitude of gratitude, in yourself and your children. Notice what they do, tell them you appreciate it. Verbally share what you appreciate about other people in their lives. This helps guide their attention to "good" and equips them to make good relationships with people who also appreciate them. Expressing gratitude is a proactive way to be a model. Do favors for one another, support each other through lousy days, validate one another's feelings, appreciate each other, and you create a culture of mutual respect, understanding, and gratitude. Every family squabbles, there's no way to avoid that. But you can model the importance of mutual respect, open dialogue, stewardship, and forgiveness as you live and grow with your children. Young people are especially perceptive, and even when they act as if they are not listening, they are still learning from your examples. Use this power to graciously raise grateful, giving human beings. It's never, ever too late to start teaching a good lesson.

### 3.1. Self-Care and Self-Reflection

Single parents could, for example, make themselves aware of possible relaxation techniques (for example, autogenic training, yoga, meditation, reading a good book, painting or making something creative, exercising, spa treatments, hiking, sports, dancing, music, or other activities that help with relaxation), voraciously consuming TV movies or series, or using social networks to cultivate contacts. Cultivating and enjoying leisure activities means becoming a little more self-reflected, reviewing one's own personality, and finding the necessary quiet moments for self-reflection. In addition, psycho-therapeutic and social counseling can be a valuable component of self-reflection. It is an opportunity to clarify the personal meaning and significance of events and to develop deep personal insights. By clarifying fears, doubts, and contradictions, single parents can gain an improved understanding of situations, develop emotional stability, and thus decision-making in both their best interest and the best interest of their children. And this is happiness, the way to happiness.

There are some essentials that are commonly found to be helpful and important for helping single parents to grow and develop as individuals, apart from their children. Self-care involves all the daily activities that are necessary to stay in good health, the continuous replenishment of life energy, and the careful structuring and balancing of life so that the burdens of life are not perceived by the single parent as overwhelming. Single parents are well advised to deliberately take time for their hobbies, for friends and family (especially for children, grandparents, and any siblings) as well as for self-reflection. Self-reflection involves the development of one's own personal competences and involves becoming more to the "authentic self" of single parents, taking the time to look back and learn from personal experiences, as well as recognizing and working on overcoming one's rights.


### 3.2. Building a Support Network

Develop strategies for when you become fatigued that you or a friend could try during these moments. Think of specific activities that you like and that can distract, relax, or help you. All available distractions should be in the same space, such as a basket containing materials for cleaning, cooking, or puzzles while talking on the phone. If this strategy does not work, try choosing activities in a specific order. Remember that you are indispensable to your children, and they love you. Often, reminding oneself of these facts can help parents better take care of themselves. There may be times when a parent is so overwhelmed or so exhausted that they need to leave their child in a safe environment. It is OK to place a child in a securely locked room for five to ten minutes while a parent goes to another room to breathe, unbeknownst to the child. If integrating individual, couple, or group therapy, your healthcare professional, such as a doctor or nurse, may be able to help you find these resources.

A dependable, caring support network is crucial to the health and recovery of all parents and children. All single parents, regardless of their education or financial situation, can feel lonely, unappreciated, or exhausted. It is essential when feeling isolated to remain in contact with friends or family, even if it may take some genuine effort. As a single parent, it is vital to create a network of trust to help take care of the children and to provide support during moments of exhaustion or depression. The support and solidarity of one or more persons can bring parents and children closer to one another. It takes love and commitment to form connections with others, mutual respect, and empathy, all of which you can provide for yourself. Each step you take will be progress, even when met with a little failure. By being open with others, they will be there in times of need.

### 3.3. Developing Resilience

Find positive social support. If the people in your life or parenting group always seem to surface a negative way of looking at every solution and advice given, think twice about taking that advice. Our social support systems are crucial for our own personal development and the success our children will have in relationships with others. Build a positive social support system, and if it's just your family and a few close friends, that's all you need. I've noticed how much less stressful my life became after I cut out the toxic people who brought me down, yet swore to care about me. Go the extra mile to build positive relationships by taking a genuine interest in the people you form relationships with. Support them in their times of need. Your relationship with them will be stronger.

As a single parent, taking time to be alone is critical. Of course, we all need a break, and single parents may need a break more often than two-parent families. Time alone may be difficult to get, or you may have to schedule that time and be assertive with family members. Building resilience means taking the time you need for making decisions. Taken altogether, resilience is making a habit of working on making good choices for yourself and your children, taking care of yourself, setting attainable minor goals that lead to long-term big goals, and asking for help when you need it.

# CHAPTER 4

# Balancing Work and Family Life

In all sincerity, though, I sometimes feel guilty of what appears to be my absolutely unreasonable need and indomitable desire to impress Nana Fosu, gnawing at my conscience and dictating impractical schedules. I strongly reject that, though. My engagements are not driven by my family, rather by the conviction that my delivering a world-acclaimed nation-building vision will always benefit their well-being and validation, inspiring them to acquire such mindsets. As my son James Kofi wisely told me the other day, "Paapa, whatever you are building now is for us, for Ratina, for me, and all of us. And even if we are not interested in what you are about to bestow on us, we have no choice but to adjust our aspirations to gear towards the new phase engaging the nation-building capacity you are unleashing, your children's and their children's orphans." With that unadulterated wisdom that touched me so deeply, I finally accepted what James Kofi was trying to tell me: that my unavailability at times is not always a by-product of my impractical schedules; our nation is primarily responsible. My daughter Eileen concurs with James Kofi.

Starting and overseeing family-owned businesses, I have no choice but to combine work and family life. The challenge for me has always been smartly achieving balance between these essential life ventures and navigating through the challenges that emerge from this balancing act. I have daughter Eileen to help me achieve that balance. She is the Head of Communication and Marketing at Accra City Campus, University of Ghana. She, Fanny Asafo-Adjei, and I run this family business. She is a committed, disciplined, and smart working person who chips in at home and office. A cornerstone of Eileen's Home is that I am the Vision bearer and Strategic Head, and I must deliver that vision before our balloon deflates.

### 4.1. Time Management Strategies

The study reveals how single mothers employed full-time use time management strategies to negotiate their lived experiences of motherhood, and how these women use these strategies to navigate their way into transformative and growth-promoting experiences. Thus, if elected, a single father can guide future research, policy, and practice in a way that will, in a strength-based manner, affirm the single mother and her lived wisdom. Future research, policy, and educational/counseling practices should develop a stronger understanding of the socio-cultural and systemic influences that shape the lived experiences of single motherhood. These outcomes must capitalize on the collective wisdom of single mothers themselves and the findings of the current study that highlight a more holistic and strength-based understanding of single motherhood.

Lerner, Nagai, & Kositsky (2019) used data from a qualitative study on single parenthood and time management strategies to better understand how single mothers, employed full-time, manage their time and face challenging experiences. Several strategies were cited in the literature as helpful for single mothers in managing their time. These include emotional organization, working outside the home, time management skills, supportive networks, intergenerational support, and co-parenting with children's father. The researchers found that single mothers develop these strategies over time to effectively manage their time. This research aimed to challenge the common rhetoric that single mothers are to blame for their own challenges and offer a more comprehensive and accurate understanding of single motherhood through the lens of lived experiences.

### 4.2. Flexible Work Arrangements

Flexible work arrangements are not an option for all workers; it is most generally found among full-time wage and salaried workers, while generally unavailable for part-time wage and salaried workers. Yet, despite available data, relatively few single parents take advantage of telecommuting and flextime arrangements. This may, in part, be a result of the negative experiences that have been reported among employees who have attempted to use these options. For lower-paid and service workers, options for work flexibility are even more limited by comparison, despite the urgent need to participate in nonemployment activities, like parenting.

In the context of single parenthood, flexibility to attend to key activities that support both work and personal life is often critically important. The need for flexibility, ranging from scheduling support to facilitate school visits and meetings with teachers, to allowing work from home arrangements in the case of illness, is a major issue for single parents that remains a largely neglected aspect of organizational research. Indeed, a recent decade-long study has found that while HR policies, such as work-life practices, exist in the majority of organizations, these practices are both underutilized and underdeveloped without a corresponding organizational culture that is supportive of employee needs.

*4.3. Setting Boundaries*

We need to make sure that our children understand that whatever the situation, rude and inconsiderate behavior is unacceptable, whether it comes from a parent or child. In training others around us to respect our boundaries, it is not always easy to be consistent, even if the consequences of not being so can lead to unhealthy relationships with those close to us. It is common for parents of teenagers to argue less than they did when their children were younger, yet research shows that a lack of affection and emotional distance can affect the well-being and emotional health of teenagers. This is particularly true when the parents are not consistent about curfews and other important matters such as attending school.

The importance of setting boundaries can be undervalued. Yet, boundaries can help to build and maintain good relationships and prevent stress and unhappiness. When we set boundaries, we are acknowledging what we consider appropriate behavior from others, and in the process, we are showing them that we value ourselves and expect the same from them. This is particularly important and hard for single parents when children reach the teenage years. As they begin to assert their independence, they might ignore the family rules or act in ways that they know will provoke confrontation. They will often challenge us to react.

# CHAPTER 5

# Financial Planning and Stability

Assess the cost of living in the city you live in, and compare it to other places you may want to relocate to. As a single parent, you may face less rigid constraints that prevent you from travel or taking your business elsewhere, and this can allow you to reduce your own living expenses. If you are living in a city with a high cost of living you may find it beneficial to evaluate the issue with your children and move closer to support systems, or to the family member that has the most available means of assisting you, which can also mean financial savings. If you are experiencing financial trouble, reach out to state, local, and local government for advice and support. In any case, try to avoid loan providers and navigate the current market before taking any kind of action since they will need payment that can lead to more financial problems. If you remain in a city with a high cost of living, consider looking for transactions that are a little closer to financial sustainability. If you do not necessarily need the higher income now, but may need it later, remember that it is easier to work harder for less than to be paid less and earn more.

In addition to developing an understanding of your own finances, it is also crucial to have a clear grasp of the costs associated with being a single parent. Unfortunately, divorcing or parting spouses who are not receiving maintenance financial support may have to constantly adjust to an ever-changing budget; some years business is up, others it is not. So, it is important to lay out the costs involved in raising your children. First, you need to create a legal "order of support" for your ex-partner to pay. Second, you need to draft a budget for the money you will receive from your ex so you can continue providing for your children as much as possible. You can usually work with a mediator to do this and, when legally approved, the financial support you receive will be inclusions rather than new income. It is essential to remember that this may not cover the costs of medical care, schooling, and clothing (among other things). So, you should develop a comprehensive personal budget as well.

### *5.1. Budgeting and Saving Tips*

Get a credit union account: Credit unions are nonprofit, member-focused financial institutions that offer better deals to their members. Unlike for-profit banks, credit unions typically have no minimum balance requirements for their accounts, no fees for their services, and fewer fees for ATM usage. Many also have agreements with ATMs, which will reduce the fees you pay. They're worth looking into. Let your kids in on your financial woes: Show your kids how much of your earnings go to the basic bills you need to pay every month. Open up a checking account in their name if they're old enough, and show them just how much of your income you would have left if you didn't spend it. Ask the banks, "At what age can I open an account for my child and include myself as a co-signer without it incurring fees?" My daughter has an account in her name, but it's easier for me to cut fees by establishing a custodial relationship in which I'm the signer that gives me control over the account... and no fees.

Use direct deposit: If you don't already have direct deposit through your employer, sign up for it immediately. It's convenient, and it will help prevent you from blowing your entire paycheck the second you get it. Make a budget and stick to it: An exercise I did in graduate school showed me exactly how I spent my income, and how much I had left afterwards. I didn't like what I saw, and I was able to cut out much of what I thought was essential spending without it being painful. Look at where you spend your money, and how much you have left over at the end of each month. You, of all people, need to worry about the size of your emergency savings account.

*5.2. Seeking Financial Assistance*

In addition to federal programs, scholarships can be awarded by universities, external professional organizations, corporations, state and local governments, and can be obtained through your own hard work of applying based on your major, background (ethnicity, disabilities, etc.), and many other criteria. Many of these scholarships have application deadlines and award criteria that are competitive and based on merit more than need. You can find information at your local high school or university scholarship office, park district or library, or by searching the World Wide Web. It is important to remember to apply for scholarships every year in case there are any changes in your awarding needs or capabilities.

The Child-Care Access Means Parents in School program or CCAMPIS is a federally funded program intended to support low-income parents in college by providing campus-based child care directly connected to enrollment in school. Students submit a detailed application for the program, there may be waiting lists, and even if you are accepted to the program, there is a fee and it's first-come, first-serve.

Scholarships and grants are available to help you go back to school and finish that degree. The Federal Pell Grant is need-based financial aid and is applied for by filling out the Free Application for Federal Student Aid—FAFSA. Students who are eligible for the Federal Pell Grant are also eligible for the Federal Supplemental Educational Opportunity Grant (which is a small grant of up to $1000 for the neediest students on campus).

### 5.3. Long-Term Financial Goals

Regarding retirement, most people – whatever their marital/parental status – do not understand their true financial needs, much less understand how to satisfy them. Recent studies have suggested that about half of most Americans may not even be able to maintain their lifestyles during retirement. That number probably is even higher for that segment of American society who identify themselves single parents. Managing the risks associated with adequately funding a retirement account for a single parent may even be more daunting than those for married couples. For example, having a partner/spouse actually could reduce the strains of market risk. Parents need to hold down more than current living and education expenses. They need to scrimp and save to accumulate the considerable means necessary to finance both their and their children's retirements. After all, women live longer than men.

Goals in this area may include financing a start-up business, retirement planning, or simply securing sufficient money so the single parent, and his or her children, will be able to live in dignity and comfort. Goals might include accumulating enough cash to send children to college; financing a wedding, or selecting a graduate school or training program. Goals also might include a plan for a new trade, artistic activity, or career transition of one sort or another in which the single parent has always been interested and would be willing to risk the resources necessary to acquire the new working skills or talent. The sleepless single parent who considers the fore-going planning issues very often is burdened deeper than initially could be detected, by the huge holes in self-esteem and pride that accompany the new life portfolio. Psychologically speaking, single individuals do not focus solely on short-term financial issues. They seek also to capitalize on the evolutionary elements that financial goals provide.

# CHAPTER 6

# Co-Parenting and Communication

There are few single parents who are not still in contact with the father or mother of their child. It seems that as much as one may not want contact with such a lost love, as a single parent, you must keep the avenues of communication open, at least in the realm of parental duty. In order to cope with your pain, while trying to raise healthy, happy children, you may deprive yourself of the very experiences and problems that would help to shape those much preferred, happy, healthy children. If you simply don't date, talk or express daily grievances to anyone, then maybe it all goes away. You become a machine, the sole purpose of which is to raise children and feed, clothe and keep them busy enough to never realize that there is a softer side to you that you can never satisfy because of their innocent faces. Is this what is best for our children? Are the personal sacrifices that we make to guide them through life for our own betterment, for strength in numbers and less emotional entropy?

Becoming a parent is an earth-shattering adjustment under the right circumstances, so coping with becoming a single parent can be overwhelming to the point that many people cannot deal with it. It is no wonder that once such a monumental life upheaval has occurred, people shrink away from going through it ever again. The mere thought of meeting someone new, starting a relationship or worse yet experiencing a broken one, is almost universally shunned in the world of the newly single parent. For the strongest among us, fear may keep us from ever taking a chance on love again. Yet, even as one struggle ceases, another begins. How does one live, bereft of the closeness? How can someone frame their life around the stress of raising children alone? More to the point, how does anyone reconcile their new role as a single parent with their own wants and needs, the very reasons to enter into a relationship in the first place?

### 6.1. Effective Co-Parenting Strategies

Florida parenting statutes allow breadth for judges, and these 12 factors to be a guide for management purposes for specific qualifications and reliable expectations when legal content is written out. High-quality parenting examines, uncovers, and is accustomed to recognizing reliable expectations for the delivery of the best practices of actual opportunities for parenting. Expressing and pursuing the reality of positive co-parenting and parenting in general, focusing back on each child. Effectiveness, reliability, and empirically founded caregiving relationships built together propelling one another in directions and smiling and laughing over what you have accomplished together, reliably!

Unity-based principles of co-parenting are not connected to who is the better parent, perceived "power differential," or perceptions of the other's overall parental skills or beliefs. Unity-based principles create a practical approach to the fulfillment of the ideal of "joint legal custody," which is the underlying foundation of Florida Family Law. The strategic approach to managing the legal requirements for co-parenting is the first priority before implementing facially neutral parenting concepts. Highly adversarial cases are emphasized as there are specifics that courts determine best for evaluating the quality of parenting abilities. Shockingly, when parenting abilities may become a relevant concern in relation to some other decision being made, people are sensitive to tone and credibility.

### 6.2. Open and Honest Communication

Women who must find themselves as they reinvent life after divorce develop an independence, which may lead to satisfaction and happiness. As a result, we will also see happier and healthier children. While engagement within the community is necessary, it is a personal connection that provides solace and strength. Women are naturally a strong force in society – combining the dual roles of wife and child bearer for comfort and assurance. With the added weight of being financially secure (or seeking to be financially secure), a woman's nurturing and protective nature are put to the test and we are later able to see the good graces that emerge both in our successes and those of her children. We test our limits on all things, and life is made harder by the breaking of a family, but open communication with our children about goals and the value of truthfulness and friendship with respect should be the goal of any parent.

As families try to navigate the difficult and painful waters of divorce, it is much easier to speak from the heart than to go back in and give more information later. This necessitates open and honest communication with the children without placing unnecessary emotional burdens on them. It is a delicate balance, particularly for the parent who was left to walk the tightrope between expressing true feelings while forging a step forward in life, but it is a necessary bridge from the past to the future and helps to open the road to happiness and fulfillment not only for the parent, but also for the child. While personal happiness is not a guarantee, there is much to be said for the personal fulfillment that allows for maintaining daily life and relationships with finesse and good spirit - which also transfers to a child's life.

### 6.3. Resolving Conflict

Samantha received the news via telephone. "Hollanny, Toccar is pregnant. Pregnant. Pregnant. My kids. The kids. The kids." "Alright. Okay. He let you know and that sort of thing. I'm going to get the baby some oil and make the bed." "I strolled to you in bits. You stood there and you cheered him on. Do you know the things that people in Chancery think of me? She does not visit, and she is producing babies. He turns his mother's life insane." "Sam, I did not think that. She is a wonderful girl. Our kids will be great people because of her. You'll see." "Our kids? He is not a kid. He's an aging man, and I don't consider the doctrine of young children, and she is twenty-five, and that is not a child or a mother."

Part of the drama in the single-parent family is managing conflict and resolving it as swiftly as possible. Our families are sometimes microcosms of the larger society with all its skirmishes, power plays, and navigation of uncharted waters. Their dysfunction is exposed by separation, and there are fewer band-aid approaches available. Consider the peculiarities: no buffer between body shot comments; access to a runaway counselor; and no plowing around a potent power stalemate. It all happens every day in single-parent families. Dissension can't be evaded and may rip the remaining emotions even more. The upsetting subject matter is difficult to reallocate. "This person is still bound to me, whether I like her or not" is the constant maintenance attitude a single parent must adopt. Try employing some of these reconciliation principles: isolate issues and fears, and they don't overwhelm and drain everything which you have. Cheap shows of reaction will amplify the crisis.

# CHAPTER 7

# Building Strong Relationships with Your Children

Again, it is important to take note that single parents have their emotions tested more often than those with partners (both moms and dads included). This is a fact of life, however exasperating. Wise single parents understand that although it might seem they are acting in their child's best interest or preventing temporary pain, their actions can be harmful. It is crucial to remember that the act of discipline is not harmful as long as it's imbued with love. Discipline, together with love, transforms it from an exercise in hypocrisy and power to an expression of profound love. Children fancy themselves as the center of humanity. When single parents offer love and care, but also discipline, their children know that they are not solitary islands but members of an unseen whole. However, getting to this end point is yet another of single parenthood's many challenges, replete with high stakes.

When you are married and part of a team, dealing with child-ish behavior is usually more of a shared endeavor. However, single moms and dads can often be too emotionally involved with their children because there is no third party present to chime in. As a result, they more easily talk themselves into the notion that a child's behavior is exceptional and that discipline should be delayed. They know that dealing with a misbehaving child will result in hurt feelings, dinnertime tantrums on Wednesdays, or whatever other form of inconvenience, so they let things slide, not because they do not care but because they care very much. They cannot stop caring and fear at some level that enforcing rules will alienate their children, placing them outside the circle of their children's supporters.

### 7.1. Quality Time and Bonding Activities

The time you spend with your children is the foundation in sculpting the person they will someday become. A mistake too many parents make is the habit of treating their child not as a young person, but rather as their responsibility to develop and guide. This is not the correct approach. Children are your responsibility to guide; not your responsibility to develop. They are endowed with personality and imagination that is different from ours. We need to act in a manner that places the best interest and safety at the foundation of all relationships with our children. Far too many parents fail to make this distinction. The amount of time spent with your child does not derive meaning, it is your ability to make these bonding activities quality ones. And please, do not say your child is your best friend. It is bizarre and a bit scary.

There is a preconceived notion that single parents wish they were still with their former or estranged partner. This is inaccurate. It cannot be denied that most single parents still deal with "baggage" from their former relationship, but being a single parent is a lifestyle that you grow accustomed to. It becomes a point of pride. It should be one of the most celebrated things in your life; you have more motivation than most to achieve the goals you place in front of you. This is a crucial point in developing a positive environment around you and your children. There is no benefit to dwelling on your shortcomings. Once you embrace your position as a single parent, you can begin to develop your maturity with your children that has been denied to you because of the lack of stability from your previous decision to marry the poor partner.

*7.2. Positive Discipline Techniques*

Children of any age who disobey should suffer immediate consequences. This implies that instead of disciplining children by rewarding or punishing, we can identify and reward their selected behaviors. In turn, children may be expected to live up to their own standards. Using this sort of incentive builds responsibility and does not force a child's will. Talking with or discussing with your child will give them an opportunity to voice genuine feelings, opinions, and thoughts and is beneficial in helping children to communicate and learn positive problem-solving and decision-making. Always seeking the mutual benefit from your ongoing dialogue with your child, and not just trying to control or gain agreement for your own decisions, will be helpful to you all. Trying to control a child creates misbehaving children and angry parents. Understanding when your child is ready for specific responsibilities is a cornerstone for developing the proper control of those responsibilities. What are your guidelines for allowing your child to become part of a decision?

Take it slow so you don't fall into the trap of simply being angry at all times. Do all you can to stay calm. Yelling stops communication and injures self-esteem. How difficult it is to avoid being angry has to do with the strength and number of the parent's basic beliefs. Developing your own anger management techniques is crucial for the benefit of yourself and for the benefit of your child. How to behave may not be clear to your child, and this can make disciplining behavior a challenge, yet do not forget they are learning.

Expecting them to "behave" is just one wish for a very young child. If we examine what we mean when we tell our child to "behave," we usually mean, "Do what I want you to do." Revising our thinking about discipline techniques may make this task less daunting.

Discipline can be a difficult and repetitive task for you as a single parent. You will need to define your goals, set realistic and fair limits on your child's behavior, establish appropriate consequences that go with each rule, and then reinforce the rules over and over again. Mistakes and misbehavior will happen, but understanding what is age-appropriate for your child, discussing changes and rules with your child, and evaluating and adjusting your own attitudes will lead you on a correct path of enforcing and changing discipline techniques and practices. Encouraging your child to build their own self-discipline is invaluable.

*7.3. Fostering Independence and Empowerment*

It was my childhood identification with an empowered and independent matriarch that made me distrustful of men and marriage. We try and strive to give our children the best example of love in its many forms: familial, marital, and romantic, yet the benefits of a devoted and loving family will allow our children to continue to grow and blossom into healthy, happy, and benevolent adults. As we learn to deepen our communication skills and continue to manage fear and the conflicts of human interaction, we can exist together, be independent, and remain adaptive to the ever-changing environment that life throws our way.

During these moments, she would call out to her tiny, angelic, napping children and pray that her girls never lose their most vulnerable and trusting trait. She would daydream about the wives, mothers, and women they would grow up to become. My own mother was the woman who changed the shirt of her elderly, only son after his unexpected paralyzing accident. As I lay unconscious on a rehab center-supplied bed, mother sat erect and pristinely dressed, moved to talk to multiple therapists. She offered beauty, grace, and kindness. She became the shining example of strength, empowerment, and independence.

# CHAPTER 8

# Pursuing Personal Goals and Dreams

This is your Kodak moment, a photograph in which one tender smile quickly devolves to tears on the next slide. But in this unstable context of chaos and sadness, you are marked by an impermanence enshrouded by a calm that is quietly deafening, like an unfeigned breath.

Now you find yourself ambushing that very emotion, fulfillment, from the shadows of your darkest moods. It is difficult to remember what exactly used to nourish your spirit so profoundly. Alone and weary to your bones, you are incapable of recognizing periods of time when even the most concrete boundaries of your life are pushed to their limits. But fulfilling your dreams, living that meaningful life? Yes, while the measure of your existence is now defined by solitude, a serene absence at the heart of your remorse, here is the moment to acknowledge that longing and its importance.

Walking along your journey's path, you embraced exciting milestones - your first kiss, your graduation, your dream job. When the day came that you realized you were pregnant, your dream life ambled down an entirely different trail, but it didn't detract from the fact that you continued to feel completely fulfilled. In fact, life wasn't bad at all. You were fulfilled in ways that many of your peers envied.

When was the last time you remember pondering your future? You were most likely a teenager or a young adult. Your years were filled with grand plans, all rooted in the belief that your future was a place of unending potential, a place where you could have everything. Whether you yearned for the perfect romantic partner, a dream career, or abundantly happy children, that youthful ideal carved out your journey.

### 8.1. Identifying Your Passions and Interests

There is a lot of sage advice offered in various books. One of the best means of adding clarity to the direction you will best enjoy should be clear and focused, just as your activities and pastimes will be. The things you enjoy will, of course, be the things that at the very least hold your interest and at best feel like an extension of yourself. Immerse yourself in interests. From them, you can branch out and discover far more about yourself and begin a more conscious journey to fulfillment. Keep in mind, though, that it's okay not to do something you don't enjoy or lack satisfaction from whatever beneficial activities you find inside and outside of the home. Recognize the genuine generosity of others and the good of service that, despite the traditional drudgery of housebound activities, your children will benefit greatly by observing a fulfilled mother. Be happy and engaged because you want to make choices for the highest good of your family!

As you grow and change and mature, so do your interests. Beliefs and goals evolve, and moms around the world are no exception. There is something invigorating and refreshing in standing back to take a moment and affirm that you still enjoy what you're doing and that what you're doing is valuable. Are those things you enjoy the same over time? Almost always not. But identifying what does give joy is hugely important to realizing personal fulfillment. Notice the quote - personal fulfillment, not simply plain fulfillment. For when we can tap into what gives us personal joy or something that ignites a passion within us, we do more than follow what we love. Instead, we engage wholeheartedly in a process that charges the very essence of who we are and what we wish to become.

*8.2. Setting Achievable Goals*

To set feasible, achievable life goals, it's important to first consider who we are and who we are not. This means reflecting on what has made us feel best in the past, determining what activities we are good at and which we aren't, and recognizing the sorts of tasks that are bad for our personal health. Knowing our individual strengths and weaknesses, we can then attempt to translate the concept of attaining personal fulfillment to fit our own structure of motivation and the skills it drives. Refusing to embrace popular conceptions of success and take risks shouldn't be taken as a sign of defeat; choosing not to do is acceptable when we make room to achieve a personalized, personally meaningful success—one that's tailor-made for individuals hoping to satisfy their core values and obligations.

As with so many other topics, mainstream discourse around the search for a meaningful, fulfilling life is so frequently couched in the language of what individuals are doing wrong, rather than an exploration of what an individual is doing right and how an individual can leverage those successful strategies in the journey to personal fulfillment. Looking at popular self-help books and advice columns, the dominant attitude seems to be that not doing serves as valid evidence that an individual is doing something wrong, rather than just not doing something a person is doing. When we demand that a person adheres to standardized success stories of engagement and self-actualization, we pamper the perfection mythos because no two biographical pathways are alike.

*8.3. Overcoming Obstacles and Fear of Failure*

The fact that mothers work and study also slips them into a helicopter shape, saying that no one is capable of taking care of their children better than them, making them somehow the omnipresent parent, no matter how costly the toll. If the findings of this work are astonishing, they get tenacious with the tales of parents who have lived the impact of single parenting, and despite being vulnerable to the perils, stigma, prejudices, fear of failure, and all kinds of challenges returned, showed implicit faith and an unwavering play drive and love with absolute certainty that they could overcome absolutely everything for the sake of the smallest and most fundamental thing in a person's life which is to love a child.

But, how can a single parent overcome obstacles, adversity, and fear of failure? First, it is important to have financial planning. There is a need to be very honest with the children. Donna, a 40-year-old single mother of three, said, "To overcome these difficulties, I have to work hard. I planned everything with my children, including finances, because they know what my income is and know I'm the only one who supports the family." Without cold feet, if these conditions show up harshly, they can be a stimulus for healthy maturation since they often happen in children with other family structures.

# CHAPTER 9

# Finding Support in Community Resources

Informing single parents of the myriad of social services provided in their community will provide the confidence needed to stand up against some of the negative connotations associated with being a single parent. Churches offer support through program resources and moral support, which single parents may need to strengthen the character of themselves and their child. Churches and community centers are an excellent place to gain fellowship and upliftment necessary for single parenting peace of mind. Community programs providing parenting classes can also be found in many public schools and libraries. Online access to supportive resources and anonymous chat groups, for many, provide needed support. Most important for a parent is to be willing to ask for guidance, seeking both the knowledge and physical support needed for survival. With individual initiative, reassurance, love, and hope created through positive associations like parenting classes and groups, and in others that single parents have so much more to gain from understanding what is most needed to provide the essential care for their child.

There are a number of resources such as community centers, churches, and extended family that can be protective for single parents. Social support has been identified as a predictive health indicator. As a single parent becomes self-confident, the security in their parenting will improve. They are able to experience a new freedom and assertiveness. A support network already in place before their parenthood has made changes concomitant with the responsibility. When the parent society is accepting and supportive of single parents, they have the ability to prepare themselves emotionally before the baby arrives.

*9.1. Single Parent Support Groups*

It's important to note that the people you meet in single parent support group don't really need to live in your area, so something that has worked really well for a lot of people is to find single parent support groups that meet in a different time zone. Single parent support groups that are out of your time zone are perfect single parent support groups for parents who rage against the dying of the night and like to use the extended hours to perfect their single parenting skills. It's easy to see why it is a good idea for single parents to use the services of single parent support groups. You get a lot of valuable information and can make friends all over the world. Better yet, you will get a 'been there, done that' sense of what actions to take when you feel as if there is no one who can understand the single parenting issues you face. The relationships that you form with other single parents will continue to be good outside of the confines of the support group.

It can be a wonderful thing for single parents who want to know how to find happiness as a single parent to become involved with a single parent support group of some kind. In fact, a lot of single parents say that they developed some of their best single parenting techniques from advice given to them by like-minded single parents.

If you're looking for a way to increase the happiness factor in your life as a single parent, it's a good idea for you to find out whether or not there are any single parent support groups in your area. Even if you live in a rural area, don't fret. There are a lot of single parent support groups that use the Internet as a medium for communication. You can visit your favorite search engine to find a single parent support group that looks good to you. This will provide you with a unique opportunity to discuss how to find happiness while improving your single parenting skills on your own time when in the comfort of your own home.

### 9.2. Counseling and Therapy Services

If personal healing processes are not one's domains, professional processes in the mental health field should take this starring role. Eye movement Desensitization and reprocessing, dialectical behavior therapy, McGill's meditation for complex PTSD, and emotional freedom technique have proven benefits for individuals affected by trauma. Professional therapy services are crucial, and it is essential that they and desired therapeutic approaches are communicated with to an open-minded time frame for healing after therapy. Often such professional healers of the human mind should be recommended by specialists treating physical and behavioral-psychological conditions mutual to complex PTSD. have established that collaboration of all the health carers, along with the sufferer, is crucial to capturing behavioral additions and exclusions caused by the Polycephalic, internally controlled mind. Variants to the identified treatment styles usually require administration by more than one specialist and should not be alternate treatment services.

This may seem like a platitude, but proximity in age is way overrated. Disposition, culture, and values are more weighted indications for correlating human behavior than numerical distance in years. For belief-oriented reasoning, the individual should know clearly how they feel about personal sex and relationship values. They could be greatly impacted by their formative objectives, family upbringing, as well as difficult life experiences. Personal strength and strengthening skills and remarkable internal assets are vital not only to get you through life but also to enjoy the healing process as well, and these introspective pitfalls may bring that to light. If the individual is good at identifying and embracing personal attributes and at utilizing their abilities, there is no reason why they should not have access to direct (self-experiential) healing through introspection after any sort of trauma.

### 9.3. Online Communities and Forums

However, discussions and online networking can just take you up until now, and on the grounds that you have a little virtual backing gathering doesn't imply that every one of your requests are met and served. Mirroring my personality, some distresses are everything except restrictive. I could peruse talks about being a divorcée and figure one of those useless men you once in a while catch wind of had decided to isolate and I could possibly relate. I could peruse a subsequent post about the challenges of starting a subsequent chapter, and relate again for all intents and purposes to a degree. Anyhow, much the same as there is no subsection for the dark, there isn't a site I have ready to discover identified with single child rearing when all is said and done that represents my concern or gives a lot of help on how I can start to chip away at it.

As the business continues flying and tumbling forward, those occasions when I'm managing the example of any new circumstance worry me and force my melancholy to emerge. Having a network close by to give bolster and input through some random stage can feel so great in those occasions. Self-teaching gatherings, divorcée gatherings, repairing family gatherings, you name it... that's the on-line network I grasped and uncovered while I arranged to wind up single. I don't know how I would have fixed some portion of my life up without those enchanting messages made by strangers and those extraordinary inquiries posed by individuals who as of now had similar encounters. Each time. Everybody consistently overcome and they carried me some place. By conversing with me physically, they rearranged everything simply that small piece enough with the goal that I can take it from that point. That got me directly out of the dark gap on numerous occasions.

# CHAPTER 10

# Embracing Self-Love and Self-Acceptance

I encourage you to cultivate self-love and self-compassion. Look at yourself in the mirror and release stress with a steady breath; smile and tell yourself that you are beautiful. Use that affirmation to genuinely start your day on a bright note, to let go of negative energy and welcome new hope. Embrace your fears and worries; acknowledge them with understanding and ask what underlying messages they have to offer. Visualize your stress in a tangible way, such as a mist, and watch it dissipate. Ask the Universe for guidance and relief, then allow yourself to be vulnerable enough to quiet your thoughts so that your heart may answer. Once found, accept the promises and possibilities that are due to you. By practicing the refining and subtle art of being, of fully living the moment as a present participant rather than a passive observer, you can learn the joyful moments experienced are catalysts that elevate the spirit.

We often find it easy to extend our compassion and understanding to others, but are challenged when doing the same for ourselves. How do we expect to be kind to others if we are not being loving and nurturing to ourselves? How do we expect to teach our children about loving others if we cannot demonstrate loving ourselves? Taking care to love and embrace who we are simply as a person, apart from any accolades or achievements, is key to unlocking our best self. As single parents, sometimes we spend so much time focusing on our children because their lives are inherently our lives, that we unknowingly risk pouring from an empty cup. By giving continuously of ourselves to others, whether in the form of time, energy or experience, and not replenishing our spirit, we inadvertently lose sight of who we are. Allowing love, peace, and approval to replace guilt, fear, and doubt helps to mature the heart and guide the soul.

### 10.1. Practicing Self-Compassion

If we are willing to do the mental work ahead of time, we will be better prepared to navigate the stages of singledom and with time and self-compassion, emerge more enlightened from having faced the challenges. So much of our growth as human beings comes out of the shadows and darkness of our most challenging experiences. And with the principle of self-compassion at the forefront of all that we do and think, we are one step ahead on our journey down the emotional highway towards self-discovery. We have been prepared to bravely shake out all the sadness that is tangled inside of us.

Looking back over the years I spent in my marriage, I couldn't see, as I was living through them, the negative and often painful effects which everything I'd been through was having on me - until I found myself separated and alone. It was only then that I noticed the impact of what I'd endured lying heavily upon my chest, filling me with grief and despair. As I attempted to make sense of my life and understand it in a deeper, more meaningful way, all I wanted was to leave behind the bad memories but keep the lessons. It was necessary for me to unpack all the sadness and look every last bit of it right in the eye before I could even hope to attempt to dismiss it from my thoughts.

## 10.2. Celebrating Your Strengths and Accomplishments

Oprah calls it writing your "grateful journal," and encourages all of us to find joy and pride in small daily accomplishments. We can all practice that. Donna Condida loves to write: "I made a meal for my kids. They ate it, and they're still alive and kicking." Humorously, she adds, "this is a proud moment for me because my mom once burned sour cream." It's important to find humor in your day as well. Another long-time TSP member, Gidget1001, learned to embrace her capability when going shopping with a broken radio. Her daughter's choice of music was not hers, but she learned to deal with it: "If you were expecting Tori Amos, you are not as adaptable as you thought you were! (I learned that too! Yay me!)" Embrace your strengths and celebrate your accomplishments, no matter how small you think they are. They reveal your unique talents, and these strengths will see you through the hard times.

Instead of focusing on what's wrong with you, set your sights a little higher and remind yourself of your talents, abilities, and successes. Henry Ford is quoted as saying that "Whether you think you can or think you can't, you're right." Without a healthy dose of self-confidence, we are unlikely to accomplish what we set out to do. Know that you are capable of many things, but also allow yourself the freedom to make mistakes, to grow, and to learn from experience. The more lessons we learn, the stronger we become. The mind is like a muscle: the more we exercise it, the stronger it becomes. Avoid the temptation of "mistaking resolutions for capability." As one TSP member pointed out, "So many single moms, myself included at one time, make resolutions about how we're going to get it together and pull things off," and then promptly fail because we expect too much from ourselves. Set modest goals and work toward achieving them one accomplishment at a time.

### *10.3. Letting Go of Guilt and Perfectionism*

From that story, I realized that one should not feel guilty when one does not do things that one has no desire to do. Surely, no one can force one to attend a funeral of someone one had never cared for during their lifetime. As children, we were forced to visit relatives who had been "declared" mad and thrown into an asylum. I harbored a terrible fear of mad people, and such forced visits made me ill for no apparent reason. Later, Mother considered me a heathen for refusing to accompany Uncle P to the center of the Eucalypt Forest to attend a Catholic funeral. Uncle J. came to realize my objections and did not pressure me to go with him to the forest, after Mother made it clear that she wanted nothing to do with my blasphemous beliefs.

I remember a parable a friend told me about someone who felt guilty anytime someone required her to attend a funeral and she refused to go. As I retell it, I realize that I may have changed the details to suit the situation, but anyway... The friend suggested that she go with him to visit his sister in another city. There were so many things he had wanted to ask the sister but just never found the time to do so. As they drove the hundred and twenty miles, they finally found enough space in the worries of their lives to communicate. At the end, he thanked her for accompanying him to visit his sister. He said that now if his sister should suddenly die, he would not feel so bad, for he had asked and discussed everything that had concerned him.